POCKET PAINTERS

CEZANNE

1839 — 1906

CLARKSON POTTER/PUBLISHERS

NEW YORK

Cézanne

The artistic development of Paul
Cézanne (1839-1906) embraces
elements of romanticism,
Impressionist, classicism and
abstraction, and is all the more
remarkable for the fact that he was a
countryman who spent most of his
life in his native region and remained
unashamedly provincial.

Cézanne was born and educated in
Aix en Provence, and although artistic
friendships and ambitions took him

north at various periods of his life, the area around Aix continued to be his spiritual home and the single most important influence on his art. Like Degas, he was the son of a banker and destined for the law, but in 1861 he gave up his legal training to follow his childhood friend Emile Zola to Paris. Here he met Camille Pissarro, who became a lifelong friend, and studied briefly at the Académie Suisse. The die was cast, and the following year saw him back in Paris, to seriously persue an artistic career.

When his early submissions to the Salon were rejected, the angry Cézanne perversely continued to submit paintings which stood little chance of success – oppressively dark and melodramatic compositions, the paint applied heavily with palette knife and brush. In the mid 1860s

Cézanne took to painting outdoors, and in 1872 he and Hortense Figuet (later his wife) joined Pissarro at Pontoise for two years, during which they often painted side by side and he came closest to mainstream Impressionism. Although on moving from Pontoise to nearby Auvers he gained a patron in Victor Chocquet, he was now more embittered than ever by the lack of public recognition. Even at the 1874 and 1877 Impressionist exhibitions his contributions had been singled out for derision. In 1878, with Hortense and their young son, he withdrew to Provence, where the most important phase of his career began.

No longer content like the Impressionists to capture fleeting effects of light on objects, he now aimed to express instead, through painstaking analysis and the use of intense colour, their solidity and permanence. The chromatic art of his final years, notably his rhythmical, harmonious landscapes, can be seen both as a return to classicism ('Poussin again in contact with Nature') and a giant step on the road to abstraction.

Success came late in Cézanne's life, with a one-man show in Paris in 1895, but finally recognition had been achieved, and it may be that when he wrote in 1903, *I am working obstinately. I am beginning to see the promised land',* he may even have had an inkling of the historical significance of his lonely journey. ◪

The Orgy

Oil on canvas
1864 – 8
130 × 81 cm

Much of Cézanne's early work in Paris was influenced by Delacroix, and extravagantly romantic. He also had profound admiration for Poussin and used to copy his work at the Louvre.

The Black Clock

Oil on canvas
1869 – 70
54 × 73 cm

Cézanne's still-lifes had drawn
favourable comment from Manet as
early as 1886. Throughout his career
he was to bring the same dedication
and detailed analysis to the still-life
as he did to the landscape.

Bathers, Male and Female

Oil on canvas
c.1870
20 × 40 cm

During the Franco-Prussian War, Cézanne spent his time at Aix and L'Estaque, having avoided the draft. There he produced this early, small-scale treatment of a subject which would still be engrossing him at the turn of the century.

***Dr Gachet's House
at Auvers***

Oil on canvas
1873
46 × 37.5 cm

After working with Pissarro at
Pontoise, where he developed his
Impressionist style, in 1873 Cézanne
went to stay with Dr Gachet at nearby
Auvers-sur-Oise, where Vincent van
Gogh's sad journey was to end
eighteen years later. There Cézanne
met Victor Chocquet, who became his
first patron.

The Château de
Médan
(Zola's House)

Oil on canvas
1879 – 81
59 × 72 cm

Médan, near Paris, belonged to
Cézanne's old friend, the novelist
Emile Zola, whom he visited there
regularly between 1879 and 1885. Then,
incensed by Zola's unflattering
portrayal of him as the painter hero of
his novel, *L'Oeuvre*, Cézanne abruptly
broke off the friendship.

The Bridge at Maincy

Oil on canvas
1882 – 5
59 × 72 cm

Having shaken off the influence of Pissarro, and not having exhibited with the Impressionists since the third group show of 1877, Cézanne now spent most of his time in Provence, pursuing his investigations into the structure of landscape. Here the bridge provides strong horizontals to contrast with the vertical trees.

Overleaf – *'There are many views here, but none of them makes a proper motif. Even so, if one goes up into the hills at sunset, there is a fine panoramic view of Marseilles and the islands, which in the evenings are shrouded in some very decorative light effects.'*
Paul Cézanne, 1882.

***L'Estaque, View of
the Bay of Marseilles***

Oil on canvas
1882 – 5
58 × 72 cm

The Blue Vase

Oil on canvas
1883 – 7
61 × 50 cm

Incorporating a vase of flowers, which
would normally be painted on its own,
this still-life is also original in its use
of thin paint, rough blue outlines, and
subtle, harmonious gradations of colour,
producing the effect of simplicity
and grandeur.

View of Gardanne

Oil on canvas
1885 – 6
92 × 73 cm

In this study of the village near Aix where he rented a house, Cézanne is already simplifying what he sees, breaking things down into their essential shapes. Colours and shapes together have an almost abstract effect, creating the impression that this is the pure, archetypal Provençal village.

Still-Life with Basket

Oil on canvas
1888 – 9
65 × 80 cm

In this complex arrangement Cézanne is tinkering with axes and perspective to produce the kind of dislocation later developed by the Cubists. The ginger pot is tilted towards the viewer, and the jug and jar to one side, while the two ends of the table are completely out of alignment.

The Card Players

Oil on canvas
1890 – 2
45 × 57 cm

Cézanne painted these companions numerous times, not only as a pair, but also individually and as part of a larger group of players. Here the many subtle gradations of colour help to convey a sense of the monumental solidity and certainty of their characters and lives.

***Boy in a Red
Waistcoat***

Oil on canvas
1890 – 5
92 × 73 cm

Rough in its texture, spontaneous in its
brush-work, this study of a thoughtful
boy, elegantly dressed in Italian peasant
costume, is one of Cézanne's most
sensitive and successful portraits. He
painted it in Paris, where he still worked
periodically, using a professional
model named Michelangelo di Rosa.

Still-life with Apples and a Jug

Oil on canvas
1895
54 × 73 cm

Louis Le Bail recalled Cézanne's preparations for one of these compositions: *'The cloth was draped a little over the table with instinctive taste; then he arranged the fruit, contrasting the tones one against another, making the complementaries vibrate, the greens against the reds, the yellows against the blues, tilting, turning, balancing the fruit as he wanted it to be, using coins of one or two sous for the purpose. He took the greatest care over the task and many precautions; one guessed that it was a feast for the eye to him.'*

Château-Noir

Oil on canvas
1894 – 6
73 × 92 cm

'Painting,' wrote Cézanne, *'does not mean making a slavish copy of the object in view; it is capturing the harmony between variously related things.'* In his painting of a dramatic house between Le Tholonet and Aix, warring shapes are harmonized by the luminous colours of masonry and foliage.

The Smoke

Oil on canvas
1890 – 5
92 × 73 cm

There is no pathos in Cézanne's work.
Once he had outgrown the Romantic
melancholy from which sprang his
morbid early compositions, there was
scarcely a reference to the emotional
side of life. Even his portraits tend to
be people who, like this countryman,
look confident, balanced, stolid.

Vase of Flowers

Oil on canvas
c.1900
77 × 64 cm

Although conscious that he was a
pioneer and a revolutionary, Cézanne
nevertheless remained at heart a
student of painting, and was not too
proud, even near the end of his life, to
learn from the master. This painting of
flowers and greenery is copied from a
watercolour by Delacroix.

Still-life with Teapot

Oil on canvas
1900 – 5
58 × 70 cm

This late still-life is no less satisfying for being one of the least complex. The almost tangible fruit, its colour harmonized with the rich cloth, its roundness echoed by the teapot and jar, has something of the solidity and sensuality of a Renoir nude.

The Gardener

Oil on canvas
1900 – 6
63 × 52 cm

Left – In this study of his gardener Vallier, who was often pressed into service as a model, Cézanne uses very thin paint and the fluid brush-strokes normally associated with watercolours to produce a portrait of remarkable solidity and depth. This may be the painting on which he was working when he died.

Overleaf – *'What he most closely resembles is a Greek of the golden age. That imperturbable calm, in all of his canvases, is also found alike in ancient Greek painting or vases. Those who ridicule his* Bathers, *for example, are just like the Barbarians who find fault with the Parthenon.'* – Georges Riviere.

Les Grandes Baigneuses

Oil on canvas
1900 – 5
130 × 195 cm

Mont Sainte-Victoire

Oil on canvas
1904 – 6
65 × 81 cm

The Mont Sainte-Victoire, which looms over the landscape to the east of Aix, also dominates the output of Cézanne's final years. He painted it repeatedly, in both oils and watercolours, and the later, almost abstract treatments of this favourite motif have come to symbolize both his achievement and his legacy.

p23 *View of Gardanne:*
Brooklyn Museum, New York;
p25 *Still Life with Basket:*
Musée D'Orsay, Paris/Giraudon;
p27 *The Card Players:*
Musée D'Orsay, Paris/Giraudon;
p29 *Boy in a Red Waistcoat:*
Mellon Collection, National Gallery of Art, Washington, DC;
p31 *Still Life with Apples and a Jug:*
Hermitage, St. Petersburg;
p33 *Château-Noir:*
Private Collection;
p35 *The Smoke:*
Hermitage, Leningrad;
p37 *Vase of Flowers:*
Pushkin Museum, Moscow;
p39 *Still Life with Teapot:*
National Museum of Wales, Cardiff;
p40 *The Gardener:*
Tate Gallery, London;
p42/43 *Les Grandes Baigneuses:*
National Gallery, London;
p45 *Mont Sainte-Victoire:*
Sammlung Buhrle, Zurich.

Published by Clarkson N. Potter, Inc., 201 East 50th Street,
New York, New York 10022. Member of the Crown Publishing Group.

Random House, Inc. New York, Toronto, London, Sydney, Auckland.

CLARKSON N. POTTER, POTTER, and colophon are
trademarks of Clarkson N. Potter, Inc.

Originally published in Great Britain by Pavilion Books Limited in 1994

Manufactured in Italy

ISBN 0-517-59967-8

10   9   8   7   6   5   4   3   2   1

First American Edition

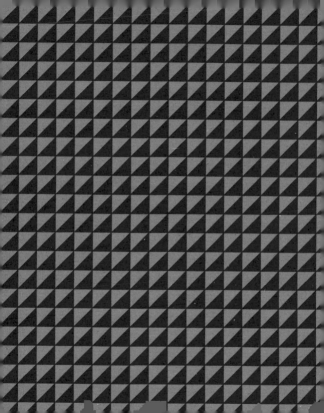